Concise Guide to Crisis Intervention

Use this information at your own risk: your physical, emotional, mental, social, and spiritual wellbeing is your responsibility. This guide simply shares what I have learned and experienced over the years. I am not a licensed professional nor expert when it comes to crisis intervention.

ISBN: 9798700249287

CONTENT

INTRODUCTION

What is it like to be in a crisis?

Everything crumbles:

POWERLESS
OVERWHELMED
NUMB
RAW
INTENSE
DEPLETED
DESPERATE
DEVASTATED

I've helped people step away from the ledge, and I've experienced death: an ever-present reality.

Part of being a Crisis Interventionist is to save lives. Through that process we lend our strength and offer encouragement, coping skills, insights, knowledge, resources, empowerment, and love (which is exhibited by kindness, respect, listening, positive thoughts, compassion, empathy, and a host of other amazing and important things in life).

This concise guide is intended to help those that help others. I encourage you to use this guide as a steppingstone towards learning more on each topic. I've made the effort to condense down and compile as much information as possible, while at the same time making it accessible and digestible in a short amount of time. I suggest reading this guide all the way through. It should take less than an hour.

LISTENING

If there is one skill that stands above all others, listening is it. In my experience half of my interventions are resolved just by listening to the person in crisis, as this often invites insights into what is going on and clarity on what can be done to address it.

While it would be nice to say true listening is easy, the truth is, it takes effort and a desire to do. Make an effort to apply the following skills whenever you are listening to someone. The more intention and effort you make towards becoming a good listener, the better listener you will be.

General

- have the intention to really hear the individual
- be fully present with them
- avoid thinking about other things or waiting to say something (just listen)
- avoid judgmental and preconceived thoughts
- your words, facial expressions, and body language show how you feel: be aware of that
- focus on what the person is saying
- pay attention to their facial expressions, body language, tone, speed, volume, and emotion
- listen for repeated words and thoughts
- make an effort to understand where the person is coming from
- avoid interrupting or imposing opinions
- maintain good eye contact without staring
- be attentive to the person's needs
- be patient and understanding
- utilize nodding and other cues to show you are listening
- open body language (face the speaker and avoid body language that closes them off)

- be okay in the silence (avoid always filling in the awkward silences)

Specific

- ask for clarification
- give validation and recognition
- empathize (try to connect with the person's feelings)
- reflecting
    - mirroring
    - paraphrasing
- guiding, not forcing
- summarizing
- asking questions that promote insights and understanding
- be supportive and empowering

DIGNITY & RESPECT

I cannot tell you how many times I have heard someone say, "No one listens," "No one cares," and "They don't respect me," or even, "They are treating me like shit."

Everyone deserves respect and dignity. Unfortunately this is not always the case with those in crisis. I have seen police officers, nurses, doctors, and even counselors treat people living with mental illness as sub-human, and they feel it.

Treating a person with dignity entails
- listening
- avoiding judgments and expectations
- don't ask questions that imply they are somehow responsible
- seeing the individual as a person, not as a client or patient
- recognizing the person as important and having value
- avoid being above or looking down on them
- don't label (as if a diagnosis entails who a person is)
- recognizing positive traits and successes
- being culturally sensitive
- respecting preferences
- being kind and polite
- communicating respectfully
- affirming and validating feelings
- respecting physical space
- avoiding arguments
- being honest
- not looking at the clock
- never talking crap about them
- talking to the individual on their level (avoid unnecessary jargon and such)

EMPATHY

Empathy is the ability to put yourself in another person's shoes and connect with how they are feeling, thinking, and perceiving. Empathy is not sympathy, such that, it's not about feeling sorry or having pity for someone. Empathy is about connection.

Even though the person's situation might be horrific and far beyond anything you might have personally experienced, fear is fear, hate is hate, love is love, loss is loss. Being able to connect with the emotion and feeling is key to connecting with the individual in crisis.

While there are many things that can help invite empathy, one of the best is to know yourself and your emotions. Emotional intelligence is one of the surest ways to connect with other people emotionally. If you are disconnected from your own feelings, it's highly unlikely you will be able to connect with theirs.

Some things that help invite empathy
- connecting with new people
- making an effort to see from different perspectives
- making an effort to see from all sides of an issue
- learning about different races, religions, political views and so forth
- learning new things
- joining new clubs, go to different churches, volunteer
- journaling about your views and biases
- taking action for a cause
- speaking up for others
- reading different genres
- meditating and connecting with deeper aspects of yourself

- working with Metta meditation practices
- working on listening and really hearing what others are sharing
- being curious about others
- self-compassion
- finding comfort in being vulnerable
- having deeper conversations
- being open to feedback and personal growth
- being considerate, understanding, and compassionate
- focusing on the wellbeing of others
- reflecting on those things that upset and unbalance you
- reflecting on the feelings you have for your loved ones and then transferring that love to all those you cross paths with
- traveling and experiencing new things
- actively practicing (you will not improve if you don't make the effort)

SAFETY

There are two safety concerns to keep in mind when doing an intervention: safety for yourself and coworkers, and safety for the individual in crisis.

Safety for self and coworkers
- avoid unsafe situations
- be alert
- pay attention to environment, obstacles, and others around
- avoid being surrounded
- trust in your instincts
- be aware of exits
- avoid threatening body language, speech, and arguing
- focus on deescalating
- park car in such a way that you can easily leave environment if necessary
- park car in well-lit area
- stay in well-lit area
- make sure your employer knows where you are
- don't go alone
- be confident
- keep positive eye contact
- learn self-defense
- keep safe distance for response times and health concerns
- do not become complacent or let your guard down

When it comes to client safety there are many things to consider.
- physical
  - is the person hurt
  - is someone harming them
  - are they self-harming

- o are they able to take care of ADLs (activities of daily living)
  - o how is their physical health
  - o medications
- **environment**
  - o is it unhealthy, unsanitary, or unsafe (holes in ground, broken glass, etc.)
  - o abuse
  - o neglect
  - o food, water, electricity, warm
  - o objects and substances of self-harm
- **intervention**
  - o avoid boxing in client – leave an exit
  - o avoid confronting, arguing, dismissing, or belittling
  - o avoid judgment, expectations, disappointment, et cetera
  - o avoid confrontational body language or standing over individual
  - o keep your voice volume and speed at calm levels
  - o be respectful and give them dignity as deserved
  - o try to have intervention in safe physical environment
  - o try to have intervention in calm environment
  - o try to create comfortable environment
  - o avoid strong perfumes, deodorants, or other strong odors
  - o don't push, rush, or force
  - o don't overwhelm with questions
  - o be honest and open
  - o no matter what they say to you, don't take it personally
  - o leave your shit at the door (you are here for them)
  - o recognize when you are triggered
  - o keep confidentiality

- o never talk negatively about them
- **emotionally**
  - o listen and be fully present with individual
  - o invite trust and openness
  - o person centered
  - o be culturally respectful
  - o respect their preferences and beliefs
  - o allow them to express themselves freely
  - o be patient
  - o be okay in the silence
  - o use supportive and empowering language
  - o create a safe place for sharing
  - o show empathy and compassion
  - o validate their feelings
  - o reflective listening
  - o be understanding
  - o be genuine
  - o do what you say you are going to do
  - o don't promise things you know you cannot keep
  - o relate if relevant
  - o align yourself with individual (you are on their side)
  - o don't assume, ask them what they need
  - o don't tell them what they can't do (this shuts people down and provokes resistance)
  - o if you and individual are in safe place like a hospital, remind them of that
  - o make sure no one can hear conversation
  - o let individual know you are there for them
  - o give overview of what was talked about, any resources and coping skills offered, and ask if there is anything else you can help with before ending intervention
  - o offer follow up contacts to check on their wellbeing

TRIGGERS & RISK FACTORS

Like a gun, when something triggers us it can be an explosive and deadly event. Triggers are things that push our buttons and sometimes push us over the edge. Identifying triggers helps the individual in crisis gain insight and knowledge. Knowing their triggers gives a path towards avoiding them when possible and having a plan in place with some new skills to use when not possible.

Some common triggers
- anniversaries of loss or traumatic experiences
- being overwhelmed
- bad dreams
- remembering something
- relationship issues
- relationship endings
- isolation and feelings of loneliness
- seeing someone connected to a traumatic event
- fear, guilt, shame
- being belittled, dismissed, rejected, excluded, forgotten, or not listened to
- job loss
- feeling powerless or a failure
- being treated badly
- major transitions (new home, school, job, etc.)
- illness
- harassment
- bullied
- being yelled at
- frightening news
- traumatic events (abuse, rape, beat up, stolen from, etc.)
- aggression and violence
- being around intense individuals

- television or news
- specific smells, tastes, noises, sensations, or sights

While triggers are things that happen, risk factors are circumstances that make it more likely for crises to occur.

Some common risk factors
- history of trauma
- substance abuse
- inequalities (racial, income, gender, poverty, homeless, etc.)
- TBI (traumatic brain injury)
- history of UTIs (urinary tract infections)
- lack of family and social supports
- discrimination
- chronic illness
- poor nutrition
- hormonal changes
- poor social skills
- poor education
- insomnia
- stressful living situations (home environment, finances, unemployed, unhealthy or unsafe environments)
- low self-esteem and self-doubt
- impulsivity and proneness to risky behaviors
- prior suicidal thoughts and attempts
- lack of coping skills
- genetic mental health predispositions
- comorbidities
- isolation
- medication issues
- barriers to health care
- cultural stigmas

ASSESSMENT

I would wager most Crisis Interventionists are paraprofessionals with at most a bachelor degree. We are generally not licensed to diagnosis, but we are able to assess how a person is doing and what symptoms they are experiencing.

Some things assessed
- demographics
- mental health history
- experiences that led to crisis
- suicidal ideations (past and present) and attempts
- physical health that is relevant to crisis
- living circumstances
- personal appearance
- behavior
- speech
- emotions
- thought process and content
- concentration
- perceptions
- beliefs
- memory
- judgment
- orientation
- supports
- substance use
- history of violence and abuse
- triggers
- risk factors
- coping skills
- future orientation
- lethality

- medications
- if they are currently talking with a counselor

While there are times going down a list of questions can be beneficial (some people find it comforting), I have found it more helpful to just pay attention and allow the individual to share what's going on, as most of the questions will be answered through the intervention process. If there are specific questions still needed to be asked you can slide them in when the moment is right. This can be when it is relevant to something they are saying, for instance: "I wish I didn't exist." This would be a good time to talk about suicidality: "Have you ever experienced suicidal thoughts?" If yes, then, "Have you ever attempted?" And so on. Another good time is when the individual has stopped their line of thought or there is a lull in the intervention.

Demographics
- name
- address
- age
- drug and tobacco use
- schooling
- military service
- gender preference
- language
- ethnic background
- contact information
- living situation
- impairments
- self-help
- employment
- relationship status
- children

Mental Health History
- personal history
- family history

Suicidality
- thoughts (past and present)
- attempts and methods
- how often and long is it thought about
- do they have a plan
- how likely would they do it in future
- known anyone that has attempted or completed
- do they have means and method

Physical health and self-harm
- how is their health
- are they eating
- are they taking care of hygiene and grooming
- are they sleeping
- are they taking or mis-taking medication
- any past head injuries
- any problems with UTIs
- any self-harm (method, how often, what affect does it have)

Personal appearance
- dressed appropriately for weather
- how do their clothes look (clean, torn, holes)
- gait and posture
- how is grooming and hygiene
- notice any scratches, sores, bruising
- do they smell
- do they look their age

Behaviors

- paranoid
- appropriate or inappropriate
- erratic
- agitated
- aggressive
- hyperactive
- anxious
- nervous
- depressed
- playful

Psychomotor

- having difficulty staying still
- pacing
- foot tapping
- hand wringing
- twitches
- rocking
- tics
- grimaces
- nail biting
- chewing
- shrinking away
- posturing

Attitude

- cooperative/uncooperative
- hostile
- receptive or open
- overly familiar
- seductive
- passive

- contemptuous
- manipulative
- sullen
- evasive
- defensive
- guarded
- secretive
- suspicious

Eye Contact
- staring
- avoidant
- appropriate
- intervals
- from side

Affect
- reactive
- flat (unemotional)
- blunt (no change in mood or facial expressions)
- mobile (rapid facial and mood changes)
- labile (excessive emotional displays not aligned with situation)
- depressed
- tearful
- hyper-alert
- drowsy or lethargic
- spacey
- confused
- lively
- distressed or anxious
- euthymic (joyful, cheerful, peaceful)
- fearful

- euphoric/elated
- congruent/incongruent
- detached or indifferent

Hallucinations
- audio
- visual
- tactile
- olfactory
- responding to internal stimuli
- endorses or denies hallucination

Speech
- descriptor
    - talkative
    - spontaneous
    - voluble (incessantly)
    - reserved
    - poverty
    - expansive
    - mutism
    - repetitive
    - friendly
    - usual
    - responding only to questions
- rate
    - fast
    - slow
    - pressured
    - normal
    - calm
    - hesitant
- tone
    - loud
    - dramatic

- o soft
  - o whispered
  - o monotone
  - o weak
  - o intense
  - o normal
  - o sharp
- articulation
  - o slurred
  - o hesitant
  - o normal
  - o breathy
  - o rambling
  - o stuttering
  - o long pauses
  - o strained
  - o flat
  - o stretched

Thought Content
- delusions
- obsessions
- compulsions
- distortions (overgeneralization, labeling, magnification, shoulds, etc.)
- hypochondriacal
- phobias
- self-harm
- suicidal and homicidal ideations
- irrational/rational
- depressive
- anxious
- paranoid
- depersonalized

- ideas of reference (things in the world referring to individual or having some significance to them)
- preoccupied
- vague
- ruminating

Thought Process
- coherent/incoherent
- disorganized
- tangential (wandering thought that never addresses point of conversation or question)
- blocked
- flight of ideas (rapid shifting lines of thought loosely connected to one another)
- circumstantial (able to maintain original thought, but adding in a lot of trivial and irrelevant details and information that never gets to the point)
- loose association (thinking goes on tangents with weak or loose associations to topic or question at hand)
- rambling
- word salad (thoughts are all over the place with no coherent or comprehensible connections)
- relevant/irrelevant
- linear
- logical
- persevering (unable to switch ideas)
- goal orientated

Insight
- denial
- projecting
- partial
- fair
- intact

SYMPTOMS

While most crises are unique to the moment and individual, some common symptoms we see in crisis are confusion, being overwhelmed, depression, mania, anxiety, panic, hopelessness, anger, loss of interest, neglect, addiction, and suicidal and homicidal ideations.

The following are some ways in which these symptoms present themselves. Often more than one symptom is present in a crisis. For instance, someone can be depressed, anxious, and angry. Also, just because someone is angry or depressed does not mean they will exhibit all the signs of being angry or depressed. And vice-versa, just because someone is feeling restless and having racing thoughts does not mean they are manic.

Anger/Rage (coping skills pg.46)
- aggressive behavior
- aggressive body language
- clenching fist
- destructive
- feeling hot
- gritting teeth
- headache
- heart pounding
- impulsive
- muscles tightening
- narrowing of vision
- pacing
- shaking
- sick to stomach
- sweating
- tight chest
- tight shoulder

- tightening of muscles
- tingling
- tremors
- turning red
- violent
- argumentative
- blaming
- confrontational
- defensive
- raised voice
- threatening
- tirades and tantrums
- verbal aggression
- verbal outbursts
- explosive
- can't calm down
- can't get past the problem
- difficulty concentrating
- hopeless
- irritable
- losing control
- micro-focusing
- overgeneralizing
- pressured
- racing thoughts
- shoulds and musts
- shutting down
- unpredictable

Anxiety/Panic (coping skills pg.47)
- agitated
- avoidant behaviors
- can't relax

- difficulty sleeping
- difficulty swallowing
- digestion issues
- dizziness
- erratic or pounding heartbeat
- fatigue
- feeling hot or cold
- headaches
- heavy sweating
- hot flashes
- if it reaches levels of panic, breathing can be short and feels like suffocation and choking
- irritable
- lethargy
- lightheaded
- muscle tension, soreness, aches
- muscle twitching
- nausea
- nervous
- numbness
- out of breath
- rapid heart and breathing (sometimes hyperventilating)
- repetitive behaviors
- restless
- shallow breathing
- stomach churning and tightness
- sweating
- tense
- trembling
- twitching
- weak immune system
- weakness
- avoidant language

- mutism
- nervous chatter
- pressurized speech
- uncertain
- wavering
- circular thinking
- constantly worrying
- detached
- difficulty thinking or focusing
- guarded
- losing control
- obsessive thoughts
- pressured

Delusions (coping skills pg.49)
- irritable
- generally able to function in society except in extreme cases
- accusatory
- argumentative
- forceful
- incoherent
- irrational
- nonsensical
- responding to internal stimuli
- word salad
- belief in something that isn't true or real
- beliefs that others are spying, following, cheating, or plotting against them (neighbors or government are out to get them are examples)
- beliefs that others don't care
- beliefs that things have been done to them (alien abductions is example)

- difficulty trusting
- grandiose beliefs (being the savior, important people love them, having special powers, the world revolves around them are examples)
- holding beliefs despite evidence of proof to the contrary
- skewing or misinterpreting events in support of delusions
- sometimes hallucinations that validate beliefs

Depression (coping skills pg.49)
- bloating
- change in appetite
- changes in menstrual cycle
- constipation
- digestion problems
- dizziness
- dull heaviness
- fatigued
- headaches
- irritable
- low energy
- low sex drive
- overeating for some, appetite loss for others
- physical aches and pains
- restless
- sleep disturbances
- sleeping all the time
- soreness and pain (joints, back, limbs, overall)
- stomach discomfort and pain
- tearful
- vision problems
- weak immune system

- avoidant language
- hesitant speech
- long pauses
- low volume
- monotone
- reserved
- anger
- anxiety
- difficulty thinking and concentration
- emptiness
- fogginess
- helpless
- hopeless
- loss of interest
- overwhelmed
- persistent sadness
- pessimism
- self-loathing
- suicidal ideations
- uncontrollable emotions
- worthlessness

Dissociation (coping skills pg.51)
- agitated
- disconnected from physical sensations
- relationship difficulties
- difficulty expressing
- multiple different expressions, tones, styles
- uncertain
- vague
- detached from self and reality (out-of-body experience is example)
- difficulty or inability to cope with emotional stress

- distorted perceptions
- emotional numbness
- feeling disconnected from self and world (murky or blurred)
- forgetful of time, events, information, experiences
- multiple identities
- uncertain and confused

Erratic (coping skills pg.52)
- destructive
- difficulty with self-regulation
- difficulty remaining still
- disorganized
- drastic changes
- frantic
- impulsive
- intense
- irregular or binge eating
- quick movements
- racing heart rate
- relationship difficulties
- risky behaviors
- self-harm
- sleeping difficulties
- unpredictable
- unsafe behaviors
- disorganized
- fast and intense talking
- loud volume
- pressurized speech
- rambling
- unpredictable
- confusion

- delirium
- difficulty staying on track
- disorganized
- hyper-alert
- mind is all over the place
- possible dissociative experiences
- racing thoughts
- stressed
- unstable

Failure (coping skills pg.53)
- avoidant behaviors
- lack of discipline
- neglecting responsibilities
- not finishing things
- restless and irritable
- depressive
- monotone
- self-deprecating
- weak
- apathy
- comparing self with others
- depressed
- extremely self-critical
- guilt, blame, and shame
- helpless and hopeless
- lack of hope
- lack of passion (empty and numb)
- low self-esteem and feelings of worthlessness
- negative self-beliefs
- not good enough
- performance anxiety
- poor outlook

- self-fulfilling prophesy
- self-limiting
- suicidal thoughts
- unmotivated

Grief (coping skills pg.54)
- aching heart
- agitation and anger
- avoidant behaviors
- chills running up and down spine
- clenched stomach
- dizziness
- dry mouth
- exhaustion
- headaches
- inflammation
- loss of appetite
- nausea and sickness
- nightmares
- racing heartbeat
- shortness of breath
- tearful
- weakness
- hesitant
- long pauses
- repetitive
- slow
- anxiety
- betrayal
- blaming
- can lead to depression and hopelessness
- confusion
- despair

- difficulty concentrating
- disbelief
- fear
- feeling abandoned
- guilt
- isolation
- loneliness
- lost and numb
- racing thoughts
- rumination
- sadness
- shock
- stuck in thought pattern
- suicidality
- the world turned upside down

Guilt and Shame (coping skills pg.55)
- addictive behaviors
- anger
- avoidant behaviors
- dry mouth
- headache
- hiding body language
- insomnia
- muscle tension and pain
- nausea
- overly sensitive to actions
- poor eye contact
- putting others ahead of own needs
- racing heart
- self-sabotage
- stomach pain
- sweating

- tearful
- tunnel vision
- fluctuations in pitch and tone
- fluctuations between fast and hesitant speech
- long pause in speech
- lying
- measured and calculated
- misdirecting
- speaking with avoidant behaviors (behind hands, eyes looking away, excessive staring)
- all-or-nothing mentality
- depression
- embarrassment
- feeling overly responsible
- low self-esteem
- numbness
- obsessive and circular thinking
- overwhelmed
- self-blame and criticism
- self-doubt and distrust
- self-loathing

Hallucinations (coping skills pg.55)
- hearing voices
- responding to internal stimuli
- smells
- sounds
- tactile (feelings things crawling, burrowing, or internal movements)
- tastes
- visually seeing things

Hopelessness (coping skills pg.56)

- avoidant behaviors
- changes in diet
- exhaustion
- nausea
- oversleeping and eating
- pit in stomach
- poor physical and psychological health
- sleeping issues
- substance abuse
- hesitant speech
- long pauses
- monotone
- reserved
- poverty of speech
- repetitive
- slow
- weak
- winded
- alienated
- anxiety
- can't see choices or options
- depressed
- feeling stuck and powerless
- feelings of doom
- forsaken
- hopeless and helpless
- lack of pleasure or joy
- negative and narrow perceptions on self and reality
- pessimistic
- poor future orientation
- sometimes feeling oppressed
- unbalanced focus on failures and negative experiences

Insomnia (coping skills pg.57)

- accident prone
- anger and aggression
- body jacked up (too energetic)
- difficulty sleeping
- excessive day sleeping
- fatigue and exhaustion
- health problems and slow healing
- high blood pressure
- hormonal changes
- irritable and grumpy
- lack of patience
- low libido
- physical soreness and pain
- possibly poor hygiene practices
- relationship difficulties
- sluggish and slow reaction time
- soreness and pain
- stimulating substance use (coffee, meth, soda, medications)
- weak immune system
- weight gain
- long pauses
- messing up sentence structure
- slurred
- soft spoken
- stretched speech
- concentration and memory problems
- depressed
- mental fog
- obsession over sleeping and getting it
- racing thoughts
- stress, anxiety, worry, and fears

Low self-esteem (coping skills pg.58)

- avoidant behaviors
- avoiding challenges
- avoiding confrontation or upsetting things
- boundary issues
- difficulty accepting compliments
- difficulty making choices
- difficulty problem-solving
- excessive attention to please others
- overlooking self-needs
- putting others above self
- sensitive to criticism
- social withdrawal
- self-deprecating
- hesitant in speech
- anxious
- depressed
- feeling like a failure
- feeling unloved and that no one cares
- guilt and being excessively sorry
- hyper-focused on negative attention and perceptions
- lack of confidence
- negative self-talk
- negative views of self
- not trusting self
- overly occupied with personal issues
- overthinking
- self-anger
- self-critical
- undeserving

Mania (coping skills pg.59)

- physical
- agitated
- all over the place
- difficulty staying still
- erratic behaviors
- excessively upbeat
- extreme behaviors
- extreme energy
- fast, erratic movements
- impulsive
- intense sense experiences
- irritability and anger
- jumpy and on edge
- multitasking
- not needing much sleep
- restless
- risky behaviors
- can be loud and fast speech
- pressured speech
- rambling
- talkative
- difficulty concentrating
- difficulty staying on topic
- distractible
- feeling like on top of the world
- highly pressured thought
- intense sense of well-being and self-esteem
- overly confident
- racing thoughts

Medication problems (not taking, mis-taking, bad interactions, efficacy decline, etc.)

- akathisia (restless and difficulty with staying still)
- changes in sleep patterns
- confusion
- drastic mood and behavior change
- fearful of taking
- forgetting to take
- increased intensity
- psychomotor agitation
- reoccurrence of symptoms
- symptoms worsening

Mood swings (coping skills pg.60)

- erratic behavior
- hormonal imbalances
- irritable
- lack of sleep
- risky and destructive behaviors
- self-harm
- some possible physical causes (oxygen deprivation, TBI, disease, substances)
- dramatic expressions
- fluctuations of tone and volume
- hesitant
- intense
- all-or-nothing mentality
- anxious
- can be from out of nowhere
- changing perspectives
- confusion and uncertainty
- emotional extremes (mania, depression, elations, rage, fear, attachment, etc.)

- identity struggles
- out of proportion
- presence of other psychiatric conditions
- rapid shifts
- suicidality

Paranoia (coping skills pg.61)
- catatonia
- decline in performance
- difficulty sleeping
- disorganized
- hiding things
- hypervigilant
- odd/inappropriate behaviors
- nonsensical communication (writing, speaking, body language)
- argumentative
- disorganized speech
- guarded and defensive
- always feeling like something or one is watching, listening, reading, plotting, and/or controlling their minds/lives
- anxiety and fear
- changes in personality
- difficulty concentrating
- distrustful/suspicious
- flat/emotionless expression
- hallucinations
- intense emotions like fear, anger, panic, betrayal, offended
- preoccupation with religious, occult, magic, et cetera
- responding to internal stimuli

Psychosis (coping skills pg.61)

- catatonic
- neglecting self-care
- odd or inappropriate behavior
- poor functioning
- sleep difficulties
- withdrawal
- incoherent and nonsensical speech
- can be loud, fast, and talkative speech
- word salad
- anxiety
- can be overly emotional or completely emotionless
- changes in mood
- delusions (paranoia, grandeur, persecutory, manipulated, etc.)
- depression
- difficulty differentiating between what's real and what's not
- difficulty staying present
- difficulty thinking and concentrating
- disturbed thoughts
- hallucinations
- losing touch with reality
- might or might not have insight or knowledge of state of being
- overwhelmed

PTSD (coping skills pg.62)

- avoidant behaviors (keeping busy, self-medicating, pushing relationships away, etc.)
- detached
- difficulty holding eye connect or letting it go
- digestion issues

- easily startled
- explosive
- irritable
- jumpy
- nausea
- night terrors
- nightmares
- constantly on guard
- relationship issues
- self-destructive or harmful behaviors
- sleep difficulties
- sweating
- trembling
- uncomfortable or even painful physical sensations
- emotional distress
- extreme anxiety and panic
- fearful (distrustful, nowhere is safe, nowhere to escape, impeding doom, etc.)
- feeling out of control
- flashbacks (reliving/experiencing)
- guilt, shame, and self-blame
- memory and concentration difficulties
- mistrust
- negative thoughts and mood
- numb
- overwhelmed and hopeless
- racing, intrusive, uncontrollable thoughts

Risky behavior (coping skills pg.64)

- driving erratically, dangerously, under the influence, et cetera
- going to dangerous places
- going to risky areas

- inappropriately dressed for weather
- misusing medications
- neglecting ADLs
- physical confrontations
- self-destructive or harmful behaviors
- substance abuse
- unhealthy eating habits (for example, only consuming candy and soda)
- unsafe sexual contacts

Some signs of not taking care of self
- chronic medical conditions
- constantly getting hurt (cuts, bumps, bruises, burns)
- dangerously leaving things on (water, stove, hair dryers, etc.)
- difficulty or inability to take care of responsibilities (taking out trash, paying pills, shopping, cleaning, etc.)
- extreme difficulty or inability to dress
- extremely hot or cold in home due to heater or air condition use
- incontinence
- living in soiled clothes
- missing or mistaking medications
- not bathing or showing
- not seeking medical attention
- pattern of forgetfulness (taking meds, going to appointments, events forgotten, how to do things, who loved ones are, etc.)
- poor hygiene
- rarely to never eating or drinking
- risky behaviors (standing naked in snow, going into other peoples' houses, driving when they should not, walking in unsafe conditions, etc.)

- unable to get around (mobility, intoxicants, illness, physical ailment, etc.)
- unsafe and unsanitary living conditions (clutter, spoiled food, wet furniture, urine and feces odor, mold, holes in floor, leaking roof, etc.)
- communication is illogical, nonsensical, and otherwise incomprehensible
- completely disconnect from reality

Substance abuse (coping skills pg.65)
- excessive contact with law enforcement
- craving
- desperation
- difficulty with normal life tasks
- disruptive or even destroying relationships
- doing things they would normally not do to get drugs (sex, stealing, robbing, et cetera)
- drastic behavior changes
- hiding problems and lying
- intense urges
- money problems
- needing substance
- neglecting appearance
- not doing responsibilities
- problems at work, home, society
- regular use
- risky behaviors
- sleeping and eating irregularly
- spending money even when it cannot be afforded
- substance use causing physical and psychological harm
- unable to stop
- using more and more over time
- promising

- saying what is needed to be said to end intervention
- distorted thinking
- feeling a relapse coming on
- feeling strange when not under the influence
- thoughts and behaviors revolve around substance

Suicidality (coping skills pg.66)
- acquiring means (gun, knife, pills, directions for train or bridge, etc.)
- chronic/terminal ailments
- dealing with acute/chronic pain
- destructive and harmful behaviors
- getting things in order
- PTSD experience
- substance use
- sudden calmness
- withdraw and distancing
- contacting and having powerful moment with others (say goodbye, get something off the chest, relay feelings, giving things away, etc.)
- talking about it
- completely overwhelmed
- emotional breakdown
- extreme depression, mood swings, rage, hopelessness, emptiness
- extreme feelings of guilt or shame
- feeling trapped
- feelings of worthlessness, pointlessness, helplessness, numbness
- insomnia
- knowing someone that has committed suicide
- loneliness
- major event or crisis happened (fight, argument, loss, breakup, death, etc.)

- major personality/appearance change
- no joy or happiness in life
- nothing to live for
- past history
- TBI

COPING SKILLS & INTERVENTIONS

Coping skills/techniques/strategies help us deal with stressors and triggers in our lives. There is no one-size-fits-all coping skill. What works for one person might not work for another. It is also the case that a coping skill can work sometimes, but not all the time.

Some skills and interventions in the following lists repeat. This section is meant for a quick reference guide to address specific symptoms by offering relevant coping skills and interventions.

Five things to keep in mind
1. ask them what they have found helpful in the past
2. offer a few different coping skills to work with
3. instruct and have them use the coping skills during intervention (walk them through breathing, grounding, mindfulness...)
4. encourage them to practice the coping skills regularly to make it easier for them to use when a crisis is arising
5. remind them that it takes effort, and encourage them to keep at it (don't quit after a few tries)

Anger (for symptoms pg.23)
- ABCDE Cognitive Restructuring Model
- body awareness to help with grounding
- change storyline
- conflict resolution
- counting down
- decoupling (see pg.87)
- deep breathing
- distraction
- do something meaningful
- encourage them to learn about anger, personal triggers, and other coping skills

- exercise (yard work, calisthenics, weightlifting, sports, running)
- find humor to help ease tension and pressure (laughter)
- getting out of triggering situation (timeout)
- gratitude
- investigate underlining feelings behind anger (lack of control, hurt, betrayal, jealousy, embarrassment, disappointment)
- journal and either rip, burn, or destroy paper afterwards
- make sure to get enough sleep
- mentally go somewhere else for a time
- music
- positive self-talk
- pressing against wall or something solid
- problem solving strategies
- punching bag, pillow, bed (something that will not be hurt or destroyed)
- relaxing muscles
- repeat mantra
- shift perspective
- talk with someone that helps calm things down
- use something to squeeze

Anxiety (for symptoms pg.24)
- aromatherapy
- avoid triggering things (news, violent television, particular conversations)
- baby steps (small accessible goals)
- body awareness
- challenge worried thoughts by investigating and questioning
- changing perspectives and beliefs
- check off something on the "to-do list"
- coming up with solutions to problems

- confront "worst case scenario"
- deep breathing
- emotional regulation
- encourage them to learn about anxiety, personal triggers, and other coping skills
- exercise
- focus on hobbies and things loved
- get out in nature
- guided imagery
- having action plan in place
- imagine positive outcomes instead of negative ones
- journaling about feelings and thoughts
- massage hands and feet
- mindfulness meditation
- minimize stimulating drinks
- music, dancing, art
- positive and encouraging self-talk
- positive distractions
- problem solving
- progressive relaxation (YouTube has some good ones)
- question cognitive distortions (all-or-nothing, jumping to conclusions, catastrophizing, shoulds/shouldn'ts, labeling, overgeneralizing, personalizing)
- reflect on successful times in the past when stress and anxiety were overcome
- self-care (pg.107)
- set aside some time every day to focus on worries and stresses, and whenever the mind worries outside that time just remind yourself that you have set aside some time specifically for stress
- spend time with pets
- talking with supportive people
- work on healthy sleeping habits

Delusions (for symptoms pg.26)

- affirm the importance the belief has with client without necessarily validating it
- avoid challenging or arguing with individual
- focus on the facts
- distraction and redirection
- encourage them to express themselves (feelings, thoughts, beliefs)
- establish rapport and align with individual
- focus more on the feelings the delusion brings up rather than trying to address the thoughts and beliefs
- focus on positive religious practices (if relevant with individual)
- give space
- identifying content and type
- investigate how it is affecting their life
- let them know you are there for them
- mindfulness
- work towards calming things down

Depression (for symptoms pg.27)

- apps for depression
- aromatherapy
- avoid bed except when it is time to sleep
- avoid blame, perfectionism
- avoid electronics before bed
- avoid intoxicants
- avoid procrastination
- baking
- be easy on the self
- be okay to cry
- be spontaneous
- challenging distortions

- clean
- consider different direction in life
- contact helpline
- creativity
- do opposite of negative thoughts
- do something you have always wanted to do
- encourage them to learn about depression, personal triggers, and other coping skills
- exercising
- feed wild animals
- get a pet
- get out in nature
- get some sunlight
- gratitude
- grounding by touching in with one of the senses
- having a schedule/routine/to do list
- healthy sleeping habits (regular hours and at night)
- help others and find something meaningful to do
- hobbies
- hot bath/shower
- journaling
- knitting, crocheting, sewing
- learn new things
- listen to positive music or tonal sounds
- identify resources and options
- making room comfortable
- meet new people (groups, hobbies, volunteer, causes)
- mindfulness
- organize
- playing with modeling clay
- positive self-talk
- positive visualization techniques
- reading

- reduce stress
- relaxing
- self-care and love (pg.107)
- set and accomplish small goals/tasks/project
- set reasonable expectations
- shift thinking and perspective
- socialize
- spirituality if relevant
- unplug for some time
- watch uplifting, positive movies
- work on having fun
- working on self-esteem by identifying strengths, values, skills, and focus on them
- have a mission statement

Dissociation (for symptoms pg.28)
- address depression if present (pg.49)
- address anxiety and fear if present (pg.24)
- address shame and guilt if present (pg.32)
- aromatherapy
- avoid intoxicants
- avoid triggers
- bath/shower
- breathing in the moment
- check in with how one is feeling in the moment
- connect with pet
- coping with anger (pg.46)
- counting by 3's, 7's, 9's
- covering self with warm clothes out of the dryer
- eat/drink something soar or bitter
- exercise, stretch, dance
- focus on something
- get sleep

- grounding by focusing on one of the senses
- hold hands under flowing water
- hold ice in hands for a few moments
- imagining solid self and identity
- learning about dissociation, causes, triggers, and other coping skills
- looking at hands
- make sure to take medication if prescribed
- pay attention to feet/shoes while walking
- plug ears and listen to heartbeat
- reduce stress
- repeat mantra
- rub hands together
- self-massage
- take off shoes and feel grass or carpet
- trace something with finger (feel textures)
- vocalize what is happening in the moment

Erratic (for symptoms pg.29)
- avoid reacting or judging when helping individuals
- breathing exercises
- create safe, quiet, private space
- minimize distractions
- exercise
- get sleep
- grounding exercises
- keep bringing things back to the present when helping individuals
- mantras
- meditation and focus exercises
- slowing down
- talk slowly and calmly when helping individuals
- touching in with the present moment

Failure (for symptoms pg.30)

- accomplish something everyday
- avoid comparing self with others or one's past
- avoid fighting or resisting emotions, but embrace and use them to motivate action
- avoid intoxicants
- avoid self-sabotaging behaviors
- do little things to start taking control of life
- examine truth
- face fears and have courage to try again
- failing does not make a person a failure
- honor and celebrate small victories
- humor
- journal
- learn and try new things
- learn from failures by identifying mistakes made and how to change them
- make healthy choices
- move on to next project
- positive self-talk and encouragement
- read inspiring quotes
- remembering past successes
- research famous stories of people failing but eventually succeeding (Edison)
- see challenge as an opportunity
- self-care and love (pg.107)
- set simple goals/tasks and complete them (builds belief in self)
- shift perspective
- stop feeding negative thoughts
- surround yourself with supportive and uplifting people
- take appropriate responsibility and resolve to grow
- talk about it and be able to ask for help

- try different approaches
- visualizing success
- identify capabilities no matter how small
- choose to forgive yourself
- watch inspiring movies
- work on improving self-esteem (research and practice)

Grief (for symptoms pg.31)
- acceptance
- adjusting to new reality
- be okay with not being okay
- celebrate and honor the one lost
- cry and mourn (it's natural)
- deepening connection to other loved ones
- engage in activities
- getting out into nature
- grief counseling and support groups
- helping others with their grief
- it's okay not to cry (this is natural for some as well)
- journaling
- leaning on supports
- look for new opportunities if grief is based on losing job or something like that
- maintain hobbies and interests
- memory board/book that brings together meaningful things about the one lost
- religious comfort if relevant
- ritualized goodbye to help with moving forward
- routine
- seek comfort in pets
- self-care and love
- taking care of physical being
- talk with someone

Guilt and Shame (for symptoms pg.32)
- acknowledge fears, embarrassment, and negative emotions/thoughts
- address anxiety if present (pg.47)
- address depression if present (pg.49)
- bring into the light (don't ignore or sweep under rug, but confront directly)
- challenge thoughts
- change behaviors that contribute to feelings
- doing things that invite positive feelings
- journal about feelings, thoughts, and origin of guilt/shame
- learn from past and avoid making same mistake
- lower expectations if too high
- receive love and kindness
- recognize triggers
- rewording and reframing
- seek support
- self-compassion and forgiveness
- set new values
- shift attention
- support groups

Hallucinations (for symptoms pg.33)
- acceptance
- act against voices to show control
- avoid substance use
- dismiss voices
- distraction (music, movies, coloring, gaming)
- getting sleep
- give room for expressing feelings, thoughts, and sensations
- mantras

- mindfulness
- music and movies
- overwhelm with other stimulus (if audial hallucinations, listen to music; if visual, look at some art; if tactile, massage or exercise, etc.)
- puzzles, crosswords, and other things that focus and challenge the mind
- reduce anxiety (see pg.47)
- reduce stimuli and stress
- inform prescriber of symptoms
- remind individual the voices are not them or needing to be acted on
- singing, humming, whistling
- taking medications appropriately
- talking with trusted person
- test reality by challenging hallucinations in safe manner
- try new hobbies
- work on controlling voices by bringing them on

Hopelessness (for symptoms pg.34)
- address cognitive distortions (not good enough, filtering, polarized thinking, catastrophizing, self-blame, shoulds/shouldn'ts)
- address fear, worry, depression, and anger if relevant
- avoid endorsing thoughts
- avoid intoxicants
- avoid self-criticism
- be fully present in the moment
- be present in the moment
- check unhealthy expectations, self-fulling prophecy, unwholesome predictions
- create positive habits
- don't give up – try something new (thought, approach, feeling)

- exercise
- explore passions and hobbies
- find something simple to change
- gratitude practice
- grounding
- journaling about feelings and thoughts and writing positive thoughts and feelings
- learn about hopelessness, triggers, and other coping skills
- positive affirmations
- seek positive future orientation
- self-care and worth practices
- set easy goals and tasks to accomplish
- talk with someone
- think about gifts and skills
- identify at least three options

Insomnia (for symptoms pg.35)
- aromatherapy
- avoid eating before bed
- avoid sleeping during the day
- avoid electronics before bed (including phone)
- avoid stimulates before bed (coffee, tobacco, sugar, intoxicants)
- be in bed only when it is time to sleep
- calm, deep, relaxed breathing
- counting backwards
- create regular sleep pattern
- drink calming tea
- exercise during the day
- heavy blanket

- if you are having a difficult time sleeping either get up and do some simple chores, take a shower, drink some tea (avoid stressing on not getting sleep)
- instead of worrying about sleep, be okay: lay there and focus on body sensations
- limit day naps
- listen to calming music
- make room comfortable (temperature, air circulation, comfort, lighting)
- meditate
- progressive body relaxation
- reading
- reduce stress
- relax the mind and allow the thoughts to go
- set aside some time every day to focus on stress and worries and remind yourself that you have already set aside time so there is no need to focus on it when you are trying to sleep
- take relaxing shower/bath an hour so before bed
- visualize peaceful place
- work on creating healthy sleep habits

Low self-esteem (for symptoms pg.36)
- accept compliments
- address negative thinking patterns (imposter syndrome, victimization, not good enough, all-or-nothing, perfectionism, self-criticism, unfair expectations)
- avoid comparing yourself with others
- avoid dwelling on weakness
- be attentive to personal needs
- be nice to yourself
- build emotional intelligence
- build positive relationships that are uplifting and encouraging

- celebrate successes
- change personal story
- exercise
- find positive activities
- focus on encouraging thoughts (positive affirmations)
- focus on personal growth
- forgive yourself
- journal about positive qualities, strengths, actions
- learn about self-esteem and different ways to build it (learning is one method of building self-esteem)
- learn and try new things
- let go of relationships that are depleting, harmful, discouraging, and unsupportive
- live consciously and in accord with personal morals
- mindfulness
- move towards deeper and more meaningful goals and experiences in life
- relaxing and letting go
- replace negative with positive self-talk
- self-care and love
- set simple goals and tasks to accomplish (this builds self-esteem)
- take responsibility for your life
- volunteer and help others
- work on being more assertive

Mania (for symptoms pg.37)
- aromatherapy
- avoid intoxicants
- avoid stimulants (coffee, soda, tea, sugar, tobacco)
- avoid stimulating environments
- channel energy to positive actions (cleaning, exercising, projects, having fun, etc.)

- daily self-care reminders (alarms, notes, calls from support circle)
- do calming and grounding activities (focus on relaxing and calming things down)
- exercise
- have a routine
- hold off making big decisions or buying things
- journal ideas, insights, epiphanies, goals, emotions, and thoughts
- keep to a schedule
- learn about mania, personal triggers, and other coping skills
- limit activities and commitments
- slowing down

Mood Swings (for symptoms pg.38)
- recognize triggers and signs and have a plan and some activities to do (also try to avoid triggers when possible)
- reduce or eliminate stimulates (coffee, tea, soda, sugar, drugs, tobacco)
- reduce stress
- relaxing
- take care of health
    - eating
    - bathing
    - hygiene
    - sleeping
    - exercise
    - drinking water
    - taking medication if relevant
- talking with someone trusted
- grounding
- taking time off to reflect
- touching in with current emotion

Paranoia (for symptoms pg.39)

- avoid intoxicants
- confront fears
- consider the opposite thought or belief
- distraction
- grounding
- have plan in place when things get overwhelming (leaving party, talking with someone, coping skills to use, etc.)
- identify triggers and avoid if possible
- increase self-acceptance
- journal thoughts and feelings
- learn about paranoia, personal triggers, and other coping skills
- mindfulness
- grounding
- minimize stress
- not caring if the thoughts are real or not
- questioning and challenging thoughts
- relaxing
- see coping skills for anxiety (pg.47)
- seek and talk with trusted supports
- take care of health
    - eating
    - bathing
    - hygiene
    - sleeping
    - exercise
    - drinking water
    - taking medication if relevant

Psychosis (for symptoms pg.40)

- avoid intoxicants
- avoid overstimulating environments and circumstances

- focus on feelings instead of the thoughts and beliefs
- have a safe place and space to go
- learn about psychosis, personal triggers, and other coping skills
- not adding to stress with self (criticism, judgment, anger, blame, etc.)
- reality testing
- reducing stress (pg.47)
- relaxing and grounding practices
- focus on the facts
- setting a schedule and having reminders of things needed to be done
- taking care of physical health
    - getting enough sleep
    - eating
    - drinking water
    - hygiene
    - exercising
    - taking medications if relevant
- talking with a trusted support (family, friends, counselor, pastor, etc.)
- touching in with the moment
- when working with someone experiencing psychosis some important things to do is to be calm, grounded, understanding, and letting them know they are heard and supported

PTSD (for symptoms pg.40)
- avoid negative self-talk
- avoid intoxicants
- being okay with emotional turmoil and intrusive thoughts instead of being hard one oneself
- stop negative thoughts and feeling by directing consciously directing focus
- breathing exercises

- carrying meaningful object to hold onto when triggered to help lend strength and ground into the moment (can be a stone, coin, metal, or anything small and meaningful)
- connecting with the moment
- check surroundings to confirm safety, and if not, go to safe place
- doing things they like
- experiencing thoughts without judging or reacting (they're just thoughts – they are not you)
- facing fears
- keep to routines
- know triggers and avoid if possible, and have specific plan in place to follow when it's not (social supports, getting to safe place, coping skills)
- learn about PTSD
- mindfulness
- positive distractions (calming music, being in nature, playing with animals)
- positive self-talk
- reduce stressors
- relaxing
- self-care and love (pg.107)
- slowing down and seeking calm
- spending time with loved ones
- support groups
- taking care of physical health
    - getting enough sleep
    - eating
    - drinking water
    - hygiene
    - exercising
    - taking medications if relevant
- take time and space when having a hard time

- talk with a trusted support
- team sports
- telling yourself you are safe
- visualizing (safe place, peaceful place, being strong, letting go, being above)
- when helping someone experiencing PTSD be calm, supportive, understanding, and patient (avoid quick movements, loud noises, excessive questioning,

Risky Behaviors (for symptoms pg.42)
- address underlining conditions that trigger risky behaviors
- avoid going out to bars, parties, celebrations, and gatherings when upset
- avoid intoxicants
- avoid people the you know will trigger you
- cultivate safe, supportive relationships
- have supports around during triggering times
- journaling about risky behaviors, how they feel during and after, consequences, identify things that they don't want to do, and come up with a plan to implement when triggered
- managing stress and anxiety (pg.47)
- identify and list consequences and negative outcomes
- positive and healthy distractions (watching movies, hanging with trusted friends, keeping busy)
- reduce or eliminate things in environment that might increase likelihood of doing something risky when triggered (have someone hold money, car keys, medications, substances, phone, or anything else that promotes risky behaviors)
- when triggered call a trusted support (family, friends, pastor, counselor, crisis)

Substance abuse (for symptoms pg.43)

- addressing underling conditions that trigger substance use (homelessness, trauma and abuse, relationship issues, pain, addiction, etc.)
- avoid negative self-talk
- avoiding areas and situations that will likely cause relapse
- building healthy relationships
- create strong routine and follow through with it
- getting rid of paraphilia and substances
- eliminating unhealthy relationships
- embrace and believe in ability to change
- gratitude
- having supportive phone list to call when the urge to relapse comes on (friends and family, sponsor, counselor)
- help others
- journal about feelings, thoughts, and what they are wanting in life (be completely honest)
- keeping consequences and feelings after relapse in mind
- learn about addiction
- work on relaxing in stressful or triggering situations (not responding right away)
- meditation
- mindfulness
- positive self-talk
- reflect on life before substance use
- replacing addictive behaviors with healthy ones (exercising, sports, learning new skills, hobbies, playing instruments, etc.)
- address any anger, anxiety, depression, guilt, shame, and negative self-esteem
- seek recovery options
- support groups

- have plan in place to address cravings
- taking care of physical health
    - getting enough sleep
    - eating
    - drinking water
    - hygiene
    - exercising

Suicidality (for symptoms pg.44)

- avoid intoxicants
- breathing exercises
- calling trusted supports
- change up environment or circumstances
- creating safe place
- creating strong support system (family, friends, counselor, teacher, pastor, coach, etc.)
- doing things they enjoy
- encourage competency and efficacy
- encourage them to get help when thoughts arise
- going to support groups
- have list of things that calm and comfort
- have safety plan in place
- honoring and celebrating personal successes
- hospitalization if needed
- identifying and addressing triggering factors
- identifying things worth living for
- inviting feelings of hope
- journaling
- learn problem solving skills
- meditation
- mindfulness
- positive distractions (happy movies, nice music, getting into nature, hobbies, art, crafts, playing with animals)
- practice gratitude by listing things you're thankful for

- promoting resilience
- remove means from environment (knives, guns, medications, drugs, etc.)
- seeking and learning new things
- setting positive goals to work towards
- taking care of physical health
  - getting enough sleep
  - eating nutritionally
  - exercising
  - drinking water
  - taking care of hygiene
  - taking medication if relevant
- when working with someone experiencing suicidal thoughts it is important to be sensitive but honest and forthright (this is not a time to tip toe around the issue, but a time to ask direct questions)
- working on positive future orientation

PROTECTIVE FACTORS

Coping skills give us things we can do to cope with and address the triggers and negative experiences in our lives. Protective factors on the other hand are either some gift of our birth in regard to intelligence and aptitude, something that was cultivated through our upbring, or something that came about due to some random/blessed circumstance.

However the protective factor came to be, it helps protect us from psychological stress and crisis. It can be a particular skill, character quality, supportive relationship, social connection, economic status, given opportunity, safety factor, or some other thing.

Some protective factors
- positive attitude and perspective
- healthy values and beliefs
- physically and psychologically healthy
- good self-esteem
- self-confident
- self-controlled
- resilient
- strong coping skills
- strong cognitive abilities
- good social skills
- good communicator
- good grades
- problem-solving skills
- conflict-resolution skills
- positive upbringing
- positive family members and role models
- physical and psychological safety
- strong social supports

- positive peers
- stable housing and environment
- pollution free environment
- affluence
- access to resources and services

Even though many of these protective factors will not help in the current crisis, we can still encourage and empower the person in crisis to learn about and cultivate these skills and traits to help and protect them in the future (for instance, working on self-control and self-esteem).

One thing we can do in the intervention is to remind the individual of their strengths by helping them remember a time or times in their past where they were resilient and able to work through a trauma or trial.

PROBLEM SOLVING

There are many different problem-solving systems. The basic principle is to identify the problem, figure out solutions or coping skills, use solutions/skills, assess outcomes, and adjust and improve when needed.

Problem solving increases self-efficacy, offers structure and gives strength and purpose, encourages self-worth and empowerment, increases intellectual and emotional intelligence, helps develop skills, reduces avoidant behaviors, increases effective decision making, decreases overwhelming feelings, offers road map to change and growth, increases self-awareness, and hundreds of other benefits.

Some things to consider when problem solving
- encourage individual to come up with some ideas, choices, and behavior options
- take inventory of current skills, supports, resources, opportunities
- try different approaches and techniques
- look beyond signs and symptoms to root causes
- break down problems into smaller issues
- consider simple steps towards the larger goal/problem
- consider skills needed and develop a plan to learn those skills
- have backup plans and be flexible
- work on time management
- be open to out-side-the-box thinking
- utilizing Edward de Bono's Six Thinking Hats
  - objective thinking
  - emotional thinking
  - critical thinking
  - optimistic thinking
  - structural thinking (big picture)

- o creative thinking
- identify positive/desired outcomes and work towards them
- encourage insights
- brainstorm
- utilize the SMART principle
    - o <u>S</u>pecific
    - o <u>M</u>easurable
    - o <u>A</u>ttainable
    - o <u>R</u>ealistic
    - o <u>T</u>ime frame

MEDITATION

Meditation is about placing your focus on one thing in exclusion of everything else. Two basic types of meditation are contemplative and concentrative. Contemplative meditation is a process of thinking about something in a focused manner. Concentrative meditation is to anchor the attention on one thing in exclusion of everything else. This can be on breathing, imagery, sensations, mantras, mindfulness, and so on.

In Classical Yoga Patanjali lays out an eight limb process of meditative absorption with the intention of experiencing Samādhi (a very good feeling place). The first four limbs focus on reducing mental, emotional, and physical distractions. The second four limbs deal with focusing the mind and refining the awareness to a single point.

The eight limbs in layperson's terms:
1. *Yama*: stop doing things that are messing you up
2. *Niyama*: start doing positive things that will help you
3. *Āsana*: work on making the body healthy
4. *Prānāyāma*: work on proper breathing and start becoming more aware of the body's energies
5. *Pratyāhāra*: sense withdraw
6. *Dhāraṇā*: focus on something (breath, image, sound, smell, feeling, mantra, etc.)
7. *Dhyāna*: continue focusing on that thing until that's all there is
8. *Samādhi*: as you continue to focus the sense of subject (self) and object (thing focused on) disappear and what is left is just an experience of sat (energetic being), chit (consciousness), and Ananda (bliss).

When I first started meditating it was an abysmal failure. I kept trying to pay attention to my breath or silencing my mind or even trying to focus on an image: none of it worked for me. I tried for years with little improvement until I came across body awareness. By just bringing my awareness to the sensations of my body I was able to enter meditative absorption. Since then I have been able to work with most meditative techniques and achieve the same results.

This led me to understand the importance of discovering each person's path to meditation. Some people prefer visualization and things that have to do with sight. Others like sounds and music to help them achieve peace and quietude of mind. Still others benefit from aromatherapy and things that have to do with smell, while some prefer eating meditations and things dealing with taste. I myself am more tactile, so focusing on bodily sensations really helped me understand and come to know the meditative process.

Beyond the direct therapeutic value (see following list), meditation helps us experience wholeness within the body and mind and achieve a positive, even blissful experience of being alive.

Some therapeutic benefits
- reduces stress
- improves sleep
- improves concentration and attention
- improves memory
- helps lessen anxiety
- promotes emotional health
- improves self-awareness and self-esteem
- generates kindness, compassion, and empathy towards self and others
- can help with pain management
- helps with emotional processing

- invites calm
- invites feelings of wellbeing
- helps with recovery

One particular meditation I share with some people in crisis is Metta Meditation. Metta Meditation originates from the Buddhist tradition. Metta, or Loving Kindness, is a practice of sending and receiving love and good feelings. It invites compassion, understanding, happiness, love, healing, empathy, and a host of other beautiful things.

The basic steps of Metta Meditation:
- sit or lay in a comfortable position
- create and feel openness (imagine being in space or sitting before the vast ocean as it disappears over the horizon)
- choose a positive feeling or thought (love, healing, joy, growth)
- imagine/visualize something that invites that feeling (visualize a cute puppy/cat or a loved one to help invite the feeling of love inside you)
- now do the following steps
  - While breathing in, feel that feeling/thought arising within you. As you exhale, imagine/feel that energy being sent to every cell within you
  - Do the same as above, but as you exhale this time imagine/feel that energy going into a loved one. Really wish that energy to manifest in their life.
  - Just as in step two, you will be exhaling the energy, but now send it out to people you know but might not be close to.
  - Same as step two and three, but this time you will be sending and imagining the energy manifest in all living beings.
  - Rest in that space while allowing the energy, feelings, and thoughts to radiate from you to all of the universe.

MINDFULNESS

Mindfulness is bringing and keeping the awareness on whatever is going on moment-to-moment. This can be a physical activity (washing dishes or opening a door), experiences of the senses, feelings (mood and emotions), thoughts, or internal sensations within the body. Mindfulness is a passive form of awareness, in that, you are focusing on something but not engaging, judging, interpreting, or getting caught up: you are just paying attention to it.

Some benefits of mindfulness
- increases self-control
- invites deeper awareness and connection to the body, emotions, and thoughts
- increases patience
- invites calm
- invites insights and intuition
- reduces tension, stress, and anxiety
- improves concentration, mental clarity and cognitive flexibility
- builds emotional intelligence and empathy
- invites kindness, acceptance, and compassion
- reduces rumination
- boosts memory
- lessens emotional reactivity
- can improve relationships

Some things to be mindful of
- *senses*
    - smell
    - touch
    - sight
    - hearing
    - taste

- *psychological*
    - thoughts
    - memories
    - emotions
    - instincts/intuition
- *physical sensations*
    - tension
    - soreness
    - tightness
    - tiredness
    - specific areas
    - temperature
    - bones, muscles, tendons, ligaments
    - organs
    - things in contact with the skin
    - skin moisture
    - breathing (see pg.81)
- *some activities*
    - sitting and standing
    - walking and running
    - hiking
    - bathing/showering
    - washing dishes
    - gardening
    - cleaning
    - painting
    - driving or biking
    - talking/listening
    - typing or writing
    - reading
    - folding laundry
    - eating or drinking

RELAXING

Learning to relax is one of the surest ways to release tension, reduce stress and anxiety, increase immune response, improve sleep, boost energy, reduce pain, invite a sense of wellbeing, and a host of other great benefits.

Some ways to relax body

- slow, deep breathing
- think of peace and calmness
- guided imagery
- slowing down
- progressive body relaxation by focusing on specific areas of the body and mentally and/or verbally telling that areas to relax
- tightening and relaxing parts of body one at a time
- drinking calming tea
- listening to relaxing music
- taking a bath or enjoying a nice hot shower
- massage
- body scanning (bringing awareness to each part of the body one at a time)
- slow, calm, rhythmic movements
- mindfulness meditation
- listening to soothing music
- using aromatherapy
- being in nature
- meditation
- biofeedback

GROUNDING

Grounding exercises help us get out of our heads by anchoring our awareness on something other than our thoughts. This can be some physical activity, an emotional experience, or an intentional focus of our minds.

Physical
- touch in with the senses
  - 54321 exercise (focus on 5 things you see, 4 things you feel, 3 things you hear, 2 things you smell, and 1 thing you taste, or whatever other order/number you want to use)
  - try to hear something far away, then right outside the house, then in some other room, now in the same room, and finally the sound of the breath
- plug ears and listen to heartbeat
- focus on one sense by exploring its different qualities
  - feeling: texture, hardness, weight, temperature…
  - smelling: sharpness, smell, temperature…
  - tasting: sweet, sour, spicy, hot…
  - hearing: tone, depth, loudness, soothing, jarring…
  - seeing: color, shape, distance, shadows…
- have a sensory adventure by having different things to experience in one sitting such as a bunch of different kinds of cheese, a selection of different sounds, smells, color variations, or textures
- feel internal sensations of the body
- follow the breath
- stretching or exercise while paying attention to the physical sensations
- tree posture (yoga) or horse stance (martial arts) while paying attention to the nine points of the feet (tips of

the toes, two balls of the feet, heel of the foot, and outside of the foot)
- observe something in the environment
- be fully present with whatever you are doing (mindfulness practices)
- shake arms and legs
- get out in nature
- eating meditation (focus on texture, taste, smell…)
- stomp feet on the ground
- hold hands under warm water
- earthing exercise (walk barefoot on earth to connect the body's electric current with the earth's)
- self-massage
- touch/hold something comforting or grounding
- take a walk
- cook and pay attention to sense experiences (smells, sights, sounds, feelings, tastes)
- dance
- intoning
- singing

Emotional
- laughing session with loved ones
- have cathartic experience
    - movie
    - play
    - music
- be with pet
- journal
- exploring positive emotions
- have deep conversations with loved ones
- soothing and positive self-talk
- self-care (pg.107)
- prayer

- touch in with an emotionally positive experience of the past
- go somewhere special

Mental
- mindfulness (pg.75)
- meditation
- rooting into the earth by visualizing roots growing from the bottoms of the feet if standing, hips, butt, and back if sitting, and whole body if laying
- pay attention to specific things (light glare in peoples' eyes, way mouth moves, peoples' shoes, voice fluctuations…)
- visualizing safe place
- progressive body relaxation

BREATHING

It seems like everyone these days is suggesting breathing techniques to help with a host of different problems. The fact that most people are not properly breathing, even those who are suggesting it to others, should be concerning. See deep breathing for proper breathing technique (pg.82)

In the yoga traditions they talk about how the state of a person's mind is shown by their breathing patterns and quality. When someone is angry their breathing is sharp, fast, and hot. For those that are depressed it is weak, shallow, short, tight, and suffocating. When afraid the breath is shallow, rapid, and jagged. On the other hand, when someone is happy and at peace their breathing is calm, deep, and smooth.

Some common benefits arising from breathing exercises
- reducing stress
- inviting calm and peace
- relieving pain
- improving immune response
- increasing energy
- lowering blood pressure
- improving digestion
- inviting joy
- laughter
- lightness
- inviting clarity and insights
- grounding
- clearing breathing pathways
- inviting emotional wellbeing
- better sleep
- deep sense of wellbeing
- deeper awareness of self
- enhanced cognitive functioning

Telling someone in crisis about a breathing exercise is not enough, you have to walk them through it as well. This brings clarity to what you are sharing and gives them the experience of it working. It's important to bring awareness to that. For instance, I might ask them, "Do you feel a little bit more relaxed?" or "How is your body feeling now? How about the thoughts?"

During crisis interventions I stick with three techniques: deep breathing, square breathing, and breath awareness. It is important to have the individual breathe slowly and calmly. We are not wanting to add stress, which sometimes can arise when they force the breath or feel constricted.

<u>Deep breathing</u> is the proper way to breathe, as it optimizes gas exchange, increases oxygen to the brain, massages the internal organs, supports healthy digestion, invites calm and peacefulness, and a bunch of other good stuff. To help people understand deep breathing I have them gently place their hand on their throat and breathe in, then on their upper chest and breathe in, and finally on their belly and breathe in. I have them focus on the internal sensations and the movements of the hand while breathing. While holding the hand on the belly I have them notice how the diaphragm naturally pushes down, which opens the lungs and causes the belly to expand.

With <u>square breathing</u> I have them trace with their hand on the ground, wall, or in the air a square. While doing that I instruct them to breathe in while tracing upwards, hold the breath while moving across the top part of the square, exhaling while tracing down, and holding the breath again while moving back to the start. Initially I have them inhale, hold, and exhale between three and five seconds, and then encourage them to find their own rhythm and duration.

As for <u>breath awareness,</u> there are many things to be aware of when breathing. Below is a list of some things you can encourage them to focus on.

Awareness
- origin of the breath
- how it feels in different locations in the body (nostrils, throat, lungs, belly)
- depth
- pore breathing (while breathing imagine the pores of the body breathing as well)
- balanced between inhales and exhales
- smoothing the breath
- quiet, light, and slow
- sensations while holding the breath
- frequency (how often)
- ratio (how long)
- speed
- quality and texture
- temperature and moisture

While breathing exercises are good for physical and psychological health and wellbeing, sometimes there are unwanted experiences that individuals struggle with. I have met some that refuse to even try: that is okay. Focus on your breath and slow it down, soften and deepen it, and the person in crisis will begin to subconsciously mirror. You can also offer visualizations, meditations, or body relaxation techniques. They all work.

Some uncomfortable experiences that can arise
- sense of choking
- pressure
- muscle spasm
- shaking

- constriction
- tension
- pain
- numbness
- tingling
- tiredness
- itchy
- sharp pains
- jumpy or shock like jerking
- vibrating
- heat
- swelling
- stiffness
- overwhelming emotions
- sweating
- intense thoughts, memories, traumas
- desperation
- headaches
- dizziness

VISUALIZATION

Visualizing is helpful in reducing stress, inviting peace and wellbeing, coping with panic attacks and phobias, increasing focus and creativity, healing and growth, and many other things. Visualization is a technique where mental imagery is used to bring us into a different state of mind. Much like daydreaming, we are pulled into the visualization as if we are there experiencing it.

Initially we use the imagination to visualize some place or state. Let's say we imagine being at the beach. Imagine smelling the salt in the air, hearing the waves crashing and seagulls calling in the distance, feeling the sand's heat between the toes and the wind blowing through the hair, watching the sun reflect off the water, seeing different colors and shapes, and so on.

As we continue to focus on the different sensations we are also relaxing our bodies and minds. This naturally brings us into a trance-like-state. The more we imagine the experience the less our physical senses distract us. Much like reading or watching a movie, eventually our senses no longer pull our attention outward, as we are totally immersed in the book or movie.

Some helpful things
- get comfortable
- set nice room temperature
- reduce distractions (turn off lights, disconnect phone, lock door, shut windows)
- think of a place (it's helpful if you have a memory, but you can watch a video or look at pictures for reference)
- close the eyes and relax (progressive body relaxation helps)
- slow, gentle, calm breathing
- start imagining sense experiences of the place (really feel it)

- imagine what thoughts and feelings you would have there
- spend some time walking around in that space
- once you are ready to return, take a deep breath, feel the present sensations of the body, and open your eyes

There are an infinite number of visualizations. I encourage you to come up with your own. You can also search YouTube for guided visualizations.

DECOUPLING

Decoupling is a technique I have personally found helpful in my life. It's not complicated by any means, but it can be quite difficult to do. To give an example, let's say I am angry at someone for something they did or did not do. I am really angry and I cannot let it go.

The decoupling process starts with the awareness of being angry and the physical sensations that come with that. My muscles are tense, I am breathing quickly and sharply, my mind is agitated and frazzled, I feel a tight knot in my gut, I am feeling warm, and so on.

I move my awareness from the thoughts to the physical sensations. It is not easy because my mind wants and even feels justified in being angry at this person. Regardless, I keep bringing my attention to the physical sensations until my mind anchors to the sensations instead of the perpetuating thoughts.

Now I work with the sensations, imagining/visualizing the energy move inside my body. Maybe just to relax the muscles, unknot the stomach, and cool things down. Or maybe to focus the energy towards meditative absorption, doing something physical, or even addressing some issue in my life.

What I have found in practice is that emotions are energy. Once the thoughts are decoupled from the emotion, it's just energy we can use for whatever we want. This goes with any extreme emotional experience (anger, sadness, guilt, desire).

RESOURCES

While resources alone will generally not address a crisis, I can say they definitely help. In most circumstances a crisis interventionist should have a list of resources available through their employer. For those not affiliated with a mental health organization, here's a few different ways you can connect with some:

- ask local law enforcement
- ask local emergency room HUCs
- contact local shelters
- contact local health care providers
- do internet search for your town or county and type in the resource you're looking for
- contact local DSHS office
- contact local churches
- contact Salvation Army and even local thrift stores
- contact food banks

General Resources
- abuse and neglect
- domestic violence
- bullying
- shelter
- housing
- clothing
- food
- gas
- mental health (anxiety, depression, anger, grief, crisis, etc.)
- physical health (medication, health concerns, etc.)
- financial assistance
- suicide
- support groups

- transportation
- advocates and legal assistance
- community supports services
- substance abuse
- assistance with getting ID
- utility assistance

Specific Resources
- youth
    - Abuse and neglect national hotline with DSHS 1-866-363-4276
    - school counselors
    - local community youth services
    - local youth advocacy groups
    - Youth Crisis Hotline 1-877-345-8336
    - Crisis Text Line (text: 741741)
    - Missing Children's Clearinghouse 1-800-843-5678
    - Loveisrespect.org focuses on dating violence 1-800-331-9474
    - National Runaway Safeline 1-800-786-2929
    - Suicide Prevention Hotline 1-800-273-8255
    - local church groups
    - YMCA
    - Boys and Girls Club
    - Head Start
    - Parent Help 123 (resources) 1-800-322-2588
    - local hobby groups
    - local free or discount childcare (also check with DSHS)
    - youth.gov
    - Safe Place 1-888-290-7233
    - Stopbullying.gov
- elders
    - APS: 1-866-800-1409
    - Catholic Community Services

- information on abuse:
  https://www.nia.nih.gov/health/elder-abuse
- caregivers
- meals on wheels
- senior centers
- parks
- library
- financial planning offices
- local transportation services
- directory for local resources
  https://www.eldercaredirectory.org/state-resources.htm

- substance abuse
  - Al-onon (https://al-anon.org/)
  - AA (https://www.aa.org/pages/en_US/find-local-aa) and NA (https://www.na.org/meetingsearch/)
  - detox, treatment, and rehabilitation centers
  - https://www.drugabuse.gov/
  - https://www.samhsa.gov/
  - SAMHSA hotline 1-800-662-4357
  - Suboxone clinics
  - Naloxone training for opioid overdose (https://www.samhsa.gov/practitioner-training)

- eating disorders
  - national hotline 1-800-931-2237
  - https://anad.org/
  - https://www.aedweb.org/home
  - local support groups
  - forums https://www.nationaleatingdisorders.org/forum
  - finding local resources https://www.hhs.gov/aging/state-resources/index.html

- military
    - Healthfinder (senior veterans)
    - VA 1-844-698-2311
    - Veterans Crisis Text Line (text:838255)
    - Crisis Line 1-800-273-8255
    - Mental Health VA (https://www.mentalhealth.va.gov/)
    - Substance (https://www.va.gov/health-care/health-needs-conditions/substance-use-problems/)
    - Housing (https://www.va.gov/homeless/housing.asp)
- LGBTQ
    - Trevor Project 1-866-488-7386 (https://www.thetrevorproject.org/) and TrevorText text: START to 678-678
    - Elder hotline 1-877-360-5428
    - Trans Lifeline crisis hotline 1-844-565-8860
    - GLBT National Help Center to talk about all relevant problems, issues, struggles, relationships, safer sex, and so on
        - Nation Hotline 1-888-843-4564
        - Youth Talkline 1-800-246-4564
- food
    - food pantries
    - feedings
    - churches
    - discount grocery stores
    - food stamps and WIC (https://www.usa.gov/food-help)
- homelessness
    - local shelters
    - local food pantries
    - local feedings
    - local churches
    - library

- o free cellphone
    (https://www.freegovernmentcellphones.net/states)
  - o national resources
    (https://www.hhs.gov/programs/social-services/homelessness/resources/index.html)
  - o Veterans Coalition for Homeless Veterans 1-800-838-4357
  - o for more thorough resources see my *Homeless Guide: Skills for Surviving the Streets*
- health
  - o free clinics
  - o discount dental or dental schools
  - o Vision USA 1-800-365-2219 ext. 4200
  - o local hospitals
- housing
  - o local housing programs
  - o HUD (https://www.hud.gov/)
  - o utility and telephone assistance programs
  - o low income internet through Comcast 1-855-846-8376
  - o free to low cost cellphone for low income
    (https://www.freegovernmentcellphones.net/states)
- transportation
  - o check local DSHS office for bus vouchers or information on where to get vouchers
  - o Salvation Army for gas and bus vouchers
  - o some taxi services gift discounts
  - o contact local churches for possible volunteers
- national hotlines
  - o drug and alcohol SAMHSA 1-800-662-4357
  - o suicide 1-800-273-8255
  - o domestic violence 1-800-799-SAFE(7233)
  - o Planned Parenthood 1-800-230-7526

- o National Center for Missing and Exploited Children 1-800-843-5678
- o poison control 1-800-222-1222
- o HIV/AIDS list of state hotlines (https://hab.hrsa.gov/get-care/state-hivaids-hotlines)
- o Youth Crisis Hotline 1-877-345-8336
- o Crisis Youth Text Line (text: 741741)
- o local Resources via United Way (dial 2-1-1)
- o StongHearts Native Helpline 1-844-762-8483
- o find health care provider (https://findtreatment.samhsa.gov/)
- o NeedyMeds: finding assistance to pay for meds 1-800-503-6897

SAFETY PLANNING

A basic safety plan helps an individual in crisis identify some factors that led to their crisis (triggers and risk factors), coping skills they can use to help them through the crisis, safety measures they can take to minimize harm to self or other, and a plan to prevent future crises.

Safety plans are not perfect. They are in fact just a piece of paper with words written on it. Even so, I have worked with people that found them very helpful in that they anchored their mind and gave them direction when things started falling apart. It is that simple usefulness that makes safety planning effective. The fact is, when we are nearing crisis the rational part of our minds are not working at full capacity. Having a simple, easy to refer to piece of paper with simple things we can try or supports to call can be very helpful.

A good safety plan should
- identify triggers and risk factors (see trigger and risk factor chapter pg.13)
- some warning signs
    - physical sensations
        - sweating
        - heart pounding
        - shallow or quick breathing
        - shaking
        - red or blurred vision
        - difficulty remaining still
        - unable to move
        - stomach turning
        - blood rushing
        - chest pains
        - aches and pains
        - temperature fluctuations
        - weakness

- jaw clenching
  - o thoughts
    - racing
    - depressive
    - foggy
    - obsessive
    - circular
    - suicidal or homicidal ideations
  - o mood
    - angry
    - sad
    - upset
    - indifferent
    - hopeless
    - depressed
  - o behaviors
    - risky
    - drug seeking
    - aggressive
    - overly pleasing
    - attention seeking
    - avoidant and isolating
- things to shift the mind (distract until intense emotions and thoughts subside)
  - o hobbies
  - o movies
  - o reading
  - o music
  - o binaural beats
  - o nature sounds (ocean, rain, flowing water, gentle breeze, etc.)
  - o going on walks
  - o exercising
  - o hanging with friends
  - o projects
  - o cleaning

- going on a drive
    - singing
    - dancing
    - taking shower or bath
    - making something to eat
    - drawing and painting
    - journaling
    - self-love acts
    - future planning
    - playing with pets
    - and so on (list can go on forever)
- coping skills
    - all the above distractions can be used as coping skills
    - see coping skills chapter for list of things (pg.46)
- social supports
    - family
    - friends
    - caregivers
    - churches
    - clubs
    - counselors
    - agencies
    - programs
    - support groups
    - internet forums
- safety measures
    - locking up sharps and guns
    - locking up / monitoring medications
    - having someone around for a time
    - going somewhere safe
    - having someone periodically check up on them
    - getting rid of drugs and alcohol
    - reducing or eliminating bad influences
    - getting rid of triggering things

- emergency contacts
    - counselor number
    - crisis number
    - suicide hotline
    - hospital locations
    - religious contacts
    - drug and alcohol programs (AA, NA, rehabs)
    - family and friends that can help in emergency
- some reasons for living
    - family
    - children
    - pets
    - future goals
    - religious beliefs
    - things they want to do or accomplish

COMMUNITY PARTNERS

It is important to recognize that many of our partners are not focused on mental health. Officers are concerned with safety and the law, doctors and nurses are focused on physical health, detention officers on safety and security, people that work with the homeless on feeding, clothing, and sheltering those in need, and so forth.

Part of our work is providing our community partners with understanding, skills, and mental health resources. While law enforcement and hospital staff are starting to get more mental health training, it's important to remember that their primary functions are addressing other areas of life. Being respectful of this and being a positive role model for how to work with those in psychological distress and crisis is as important as working directly with those in crisis.

I have worked with many people in crisis who have complained about how officers or hospital staff have mistreated them. While sometimes this is simply because the officer, nurse, or doctor has no patience for those in crisis, in reality it's often the case that they have many other responsibilities and don't have the necessary time to help someone in crisis: that's where we come in. Helping someone in crisis can sometimes take hours or even days.

Building positive and effective relationships with community partners is all about recognizing the part each of us play in working with those in crisis. Helping community partners understand our function is important not only in setting specific boundaries, but also in helping them understand how and when to call us. As an interventionist I am not one to give medical advice or restrain someone. At the same time it is not the ER doctor's or nurse's job to sit hours with someone in crisis and connect them with outside resources, nor is it the officer's job to sit with individuals and work with them through whatever is going on. That's what we do.

Beyond connecting with community partners and letting them know what we do as interventionists, some other things that help cultivate positive relationships are:

- being respectful and kind
- listening and seeking understanding
- recognizing our partners' responsibilities
- not telling them how to do their job
- being honest and straight forward
- being positive and encouraging
- showing appreciation
- being punctual
- sticking with our word
- knowing what we are doing
- cultivating open and clear communication
- including them when relevant (cultivate teamwork)
- being a positive example when it comes to working with those in crisis
- avoiding gossip
- setting proper boundaries
- being willing to ask for help when needed
- being consistent
- knowing rules and guidelines
- knowing and sharing resources
- avoiding confrontation and when conflict arises to not address it in front of the person in crisis
- avoiding blame and accusations
- not blindsiding or dumping responsibilities onto them
- asking and showing interest in their work and lives
- networking and involving yourself in partner events that you've been invited to
- speaking highly of community partners to others

RANDOM THOUGHTS

Encouragement and Empowerment

While this guide is focused on helping those that work with people in crisis, it's also about encouraging self-knowledge and empowerment for all involved.

Here's an empowering experience I had in my troubled youth.

I was thirteen, sitting across from my adopted parents that I hadn't seen for months. The social worker was to the side, as if in shadow, because all I could see was my adopted mom crying and seeking comfort from someone that betrayed and left her years before.

Everything was muffled,
like my ears were plugged up.

Then pop.

Reality hit.

"This is the last time you'll see us," my adopted dad said.

Sounds of gut-wrenching tears echo in my mind even today.

I remember the social worker standing in front of me:
protected
insolated
fabric was all I saw.

She ushered me out with a gentle loving hand on my shoulder: it shook.

Months later she stopped trying to fix me and started to teach me. For months I told her what she wanted to hear, for I'd long gotten used to telling people what they wanted to hear, and she knew it. She called me on my shit and started teaching me psychology.

She taught me to fix myself.

It's been 32 years and I'm still working on it ☺

My Process

When I want to change something I take a conscious moment or moments to focus on whatever is going on. I give the emotions and thoughts room to express themselves. I learn everything I can on the topic. For instance, if I am dealing with anxiety I will do a bunch of research on anxiety. I will also look back in my life and try to remember any major moments of anxiety I had experienced. After that, I work on transforming and processing through whatever it is that comes up.

Usually my process entails creating a sacred space, eliminate all distractions, and meditating on whatever it is that I am working on. All thoughts are focused on the problem until insights and clarity arise. It's those insights and my concerted effort towards healing and growth that ultimately brings about positive change. I can honestly say it's hard to change. Anyone that says otherwise is lying, doesn't know, or is trying to sell us something. Thankfully, the more you work at it, the easier it gets.

If you want to grow and have more control over your life it is essential that you process through negative experiences, memories, and traumas.

Some things that help
- journal
- talk with someone
- re-write experience in an empowering light
- find something of value to take away from experience
- help others
- join support group
- work on being with traumatic memory without it affecting breath or body
- allow yourself to feel the pain instead of avoiding, hiding, or ignoring
- avoid self-degrading thoughts or what-ifs
- avoid taking on too much: work with a little bit of the energy at a time
- avoid escapism such as substance use
- self-care (pg.107)
- make sure to get sleep
- exercise
- work with cognitive-behavior therapies
- work with mindfulness based stress reduction therapies
- give yourself time to think about and process experience
- work on grounding and being present with what is in the now
- connect with the emotion and any related body sensations or areas
- redefining yourself
- find a higher level of self-integration
- seek and enjoy happiness
- find spiritual fulfillment

It's gotta be more than a paycheck

Working in this field has got to be more than a check because the pay isn't much. I feel it is important to ask yourself, "Why am I doing it?"

For me it was originally about the paycheck and getting off my back after a major accident. Since then I have gained so much more.

Some unwanted things I've had to face
- anger
- bitterness
- anxiety
- paranoia
- fear
- sadness
- burnout
- compassion fatigue
- secondary trauma
- death
- threats to my life

Some wanted things
- healing
- strength and empowerment
- transformation
- certainty
- becoming a more attentive husband and father
- deeper sense of self
- learning about self-care

Some gifts
- healing others
- saving lives
- transforming lives
- connecting with amazing people
- learning and growing

There is a lot of turnover in the mental health field. Some reasons for this are being overwhelmed, burnout, compassion fatigue, excessive paperwork, issues with the system, conflict with those in crisis, being triggered, and being unable to deal with the intensity in general.

I encourage you to find a deeper reason to work in this field beyond the paycheck. If this is for personal growth, to help others, or some other thing, figure it out. Otherwise, the odds are in a year or two you will likely get burned out and disillusioned. The fact is, this is not an easy field to work in.

While there are successes, there are also many failures and many tragic stories that will bring you to tears and keep you up at night. To help with those things see section on self-care (pg.107)

The reason why I am pointing this out is because it's real. Helping people through crisis is emotionally and mentally difficult and draining. Having a bigger purpose than getting paid makes a huge difference.

Paperwork

I have never heard of anyone speak highly of paperwork: not CEOs, doctors, nurses, counselors, managers, teachers, or interventionists. Why? Because it sucks.

I have to be honest, as of this writing I still struggle with it. I know some of it is good in order to help track how clients are doing and what things are and are not helping, but for the most part, it's redundant bullshit that needs to be done in order for our companies and ourselves to get paid.

I have learned over the years to just do it as soon as possible. Letting things slide always creates more stress and work in the end. I have even seen people get fired because they were behind in their paperwork.

While it is stressful, annoying, and sometimes even infuriating, it has to be done. My advice to you, accept that it needs to be done and do it as soon as you can.

Believe in yourself and be okay with not knowing

Paperwork and talking with those in crisis are two big things that at first are very challenging. Paperwork and learning your company's software just takes time. Don't stress about it. Just know that at first it will be overwhelming and difficult. The more you do it, the easier it gets.

As for talking with those in crisis, that gets easier with time as well. Some things that will help you become more comfortable with that are learning to listen, knowing resources, and offering coping skills. Those three things are your greatest tools in helping people in crisis. There will be times though when there is no easy solution. I have sat there with nothing to say. I have even said things like, "Woah, I don't know what to say." We are not expected to have a solution for every situation. Sometimes just being there for the person is all we can do.

Other times we have to refer them to others. While it might seem like we are alone, the truth is, we're not. We have our coworkers and partners to lean on.

Knowing what we can and cannot do is very important in helping us gain confidence in ourselves. The more you believe in yourself, the more you will be able to help those in crisis.

What matters is that you keep refining yourself until you find your groove.

Mandated Reporting

Physical, mental, emotional, and sexual abuse, neglect, unsafe environments, and being gravely disabled are all cases in which we need to report to outside agencies. I work in Washington State, so I report abuses to Child Protected Services (CPS) and Adult Protective Services (APS), and with people that are gravely disabled or unable to safety plan to Designated Crisis Responders (DCRs).

Things we need to report
- extent, duration, and nature of situation
- known times and dates
- date of report
- perpetrator's information and relationship to victim
- victim's information
- reporter's information (name, agency, position, and contact info)

While it is absolutely necessary and easy to report child and elder abuse, there are times when reporting sucks because it makes things worse. For instance, someone is in crisis and they say something like, "I could just kill them." There is no plan, means, or real intent. The person is just expressing how they feel in the moment. Heck, I've had similar passing thoughts in my life. Even so, we still have to report it. There is always the possibility that a person will act on their thoughts, so it is always better to be safe than sorry.

SELF-CARE

You would think people in the mental health field would naturally take care of their mental health, but this is not always the case. With all the normal stressors in life, working with those in crisis can really affect our wellbeing. Unless you purposely set aside some time for self-care, the odds are, life is moving too quickly and intensely to focus on it.

While there are millions of self-caring things you can do, one of the most important is to purposely set aside some time to be fully conscious of the act of self-care and love. It is that reflective aspect of "doing" that has a stronger effect. If you mindlessly do self-care, it will have an effect, but not as strong as when you consciously do it with intentional purpose.

Having worked in the mental health field for nearly eight years, five of them being in crisis, I have experienced secondary and vicarious trauma, transference, burnout, compassion fatigue, paperwork rebellion, overwork due to turnovers, exhaustion, insomnia and fatigue, unbearable sadness over peoples' experiences, death threats, seen a dead body, experienced anger and frustration, indifference, and delirium (I work graveyard shifts).

It is no wonder the mental health field has a huge turnover rate. Besides the experiences I've had when working with those in need, there is never enough money to pay employees adequately or to hire more people, which in turn creates a situation where clinicians and interventionists are overwhelmed with the number of people they are trying to help. On top of that, there are limited resources. If we add mental health stigmas, sometimes being projected on and hurtful things said to us, and an excessive amount of paperwork, you can start to understand why so many people leave.

Therefore, it is important to recognize the early signs of fatigue, burnout, and trauma that arise, and to address them before they negatively impact your mental health and wellbeing.

Signs of compassion fatigue
- indifferent and apathetic
- exhaustion
- depersonalized
- irritable and impatient
- contempt towards self and others
- sleeping difficulty
- weight loss or gain
- burnout
- bottling up emotions
- overly burdened
- isolation
- loss of pleasure
- concentration problems
- hopeless
- powerless
- drug and alcohol use
- detached
- judgmental
- intolerant
- bitter
- pessimistic

Signs of secondary and vicarious trauma
- frustration and anger
- anxiety and panic
- irritability
- fear
- sleeping difficulties (insomnia, nightmares, restlessness)

- exhaustion and fatigue
- invasive thoughts
- changes in beliefs and perceptions of life
- distress
- isolation
- guilt and shame
- self-blame
- sexual problems
- relationship problems
- argumentative
- hopelessness
- loss of pleasure and happiness
- disorientation and confusion
- mood swings
- overwhelming emotions
- replaying traumas and stories
- memory problems
- easily startled
- difficulty leaving behind work

Signs of burnout
- not satisfied with work
- complaining
- stressed out
- frustrated and irritable
- overwhelmed and pressured
- feeling powerless
- not taking breaks
- lack of energy
- difficulty concentrating or staying on task
- stealing
- destruction of property
- surfing the web

- physically tense
- physical issues (headaches, stomach problems, soreness)
- feeling useless
- disillusioned
- emotionally stressed
- blaming
- gossiping
- depression
- anxiety
- loss of appetite
- risky behaviors
- drug and alcohol abuse
- apathy
- hopeless
- cynicism
- critical
- doing things half-ass
- illness
- negative thoughts toward work, coworkers, administration

The following is a basic list of things you can do to reduce and help with burnout, fatigue, and trauma. For more things you can do see coping skills chapter (pg. 46).

Physical self-care
- exercising
- dancing
- gardening
- getting enough sleep
- taking care of hygiene
- eating healthy and balanced meals
- drinking water

- reducing unhealthy habits and consumptions
- work on time management
- get a massage
- treat yourself to something nice (ice cream works for me ☺)
- recognize limits
- do things you enjoy

Emotional self-care
- journaling and processing
- cathartic movies
- get into nature (beach, mountains, rivers, forests)
- laughing
- socializing with friends
- debriefing after intense interactions
- support groups
- doing things you enjoy

Mental self-care
- learn new things
- hobbies
- puzzles and mysteries
- improve memory skills
- work on concentration exercises
- reading
- talking with someone

Spiritual self-care
- church or other spiritual organization
- meditation
- getting out in nature
- doing ritual

While it would be ideal to work with self-care daily, the truth is, this is not always going to happen. I encourage you though to set aside some time every week to do some self-care. Humans are creatures of habit. By intentionally setting aside some time each day/week, it will eventually become second nature.

Just remember to be fully present and aware while doing it. Don't let it become another mindless robotic thing you do. Make it special. Light a candle, some incense, say a prayer or affirmation, make it special, and it will be special and way more powerful than just going through the motions.

CRISIS INTERVENTION MODELS

There are a few different crisis models out there. All of them aim to help individuals out of crisis by assessing the situation and needs, listening to what they are saying and expressing, offering supports and coping skills, and connecting them with other resources. Here are a few different models to consider.

Albert Roberts SAFER-R Model
1. <u>S</u>tabilize
2. <u>A</u>cknowledge
3. <u>F</u>acilitate understanding
4. <u>E</u>ducate and <u>E</u>ncourage coping skills
5. <u>R</u>estore function
6. <u>R</u>efer to other services

Kristi Kanel's ABC Model
1. <u>A</u>ligning with individual and establishing/maintaining rapport
2. <u>B</u>reaking down problem (identify triggers, stressors, risk factors, symptoms, needs, crisis)
3. <u>C</u>oping

Albert Robert's ACT Model
1. <u>A</u>ssessment
2. <u>C</u>risis Intervention
3. <u>T</u>rauma Treatment

Jackson-Cherry's and Erford's ABCDE Model
1. <u>A</u>ffect: how is person doing
2. <u>B</u>ehaviors: what are they doing
3. <u>C</u>ognitions: what are they thinking
4. <u>D</u>evelopment: developing skills and resources
5. <u>E</u>nvironment: what conditions and background are they coming from

Mental Health First Aid Action Plan (ALGEE)
1. Assess for risk of suicide or harm
2. Listen nonjudgmentally
3. Give reassurance and information
4. Encourage appropriate professional help
5. Encourage self-help and other supportive strategies as well as Empower

Edward's and Jones' ABCD Model
1. Achieve contact and rapport
2. Boil down problem
3. Cope with problem
4. Determine meaning from event

National Child Traumatic Stress Network's Psychological First Aid (PFA)
1. Contact and engage
2. Safety and comfort
3. Stabilization
4. Identifying needs and concerns
5. Practical assistance
6. Connecting with social supports
7. Coping skills
8. Linking with collaborating services

MacDonald's Six Step Model
1. Defining the problem
2. Ensuring safety
3. Providing support
4. Examine alternatives
5. Making plans
6. Obtaining commitment

REFERENCES

American Psychiatric Association. *Diagnostic and Statistical Manual of Mental Disorders, 5th edition*. American Psychiatric Publishing, 2013.

Cavaiola, Alan A., and Joseph E. Colford. *Crisis Intervention: a Practical Guide*. SAGE, 2018.

Jackson-Cherry, Lisa R., and Bradley T. Erford. *Crisis Assessment, Intervention, and Prevention*. Pearson, 2018.

Haddad, Fadi, and Ruth Gerson. *Helping Kids in Crisis: Managing Psychiatric Emergencies in Children and Adolescents*. American Psychiatric Publishing, 2015.

Halloran, Janine. *Coping Skills for Kids Workbook: over 75 Coping Strategies to Help Kids Deal with Stress, Anxiety and Anger*. PESI Publishing & Media, 2018.

Gilliland, Burl E., and Richard K. James. *Crisis Intervention Strategies*. Thomson Brooks/Cole, 2005.

Kanel, Kristi. *A Guide to Crisis Intervention*. Cengage, 2018.

Roberts, Albert R., and Kenneth Yeager. *Pocket Guide to Crisis Intervention*. Oxford University Press, 2009.

Snider, Leslie, et al. *Psychological First Aid: Guide for Field Workers*. World Health Organization, 2011.

Yeager, Kenneth, and Albert R. Roberts. *Crisis Intervention Handbook: Assessment, Treatment, and Research*. Oxford University Press, 2015.

INDEX

MY WRITINGS

Guide for the Homeless: Skills for Surviving the Streets

This guide focuses on physical and emotional skills needed to survive and thrive on the streets. Some things talked about are finding shelter and food, remaining safe and healthy, learning how to make money, and how to take care of emotional wellbeing.

Concise Guide to Companion Planting

This is my first of a series of gardening guides. In this guide I talk about different plant combinations to help protect, shelter, or strengthen the vegetable garden. I also talk about planting specific flowers to invite beneficial insects and encourage diversity. The guide ends with a list of plant characteristics, planting times, growth habits, and beneficial and harmful plants to grow or avoid growing with vegetables.

Concise Guide to Climate Change

This guide lists evidence of climate change and gives a thorough list of things we can do to help reduce and eliminate further worsening of the problem.

A Different Road: From Bum to Mystic

This book shares some experiences I had while traveling and living on the streets.

ABOUT AUTHOR

I've worked in the mental health field for more than eight years, five of which have been in Crisis. I spend my free time homeschooling my children, gardening, hiking, chasing chickens, dancing with my wife, and enjoying life.